WHITE QUEEN'S LAST STAND

POEMS ON THE LIFE
AND WORK OF
GERMAINE RICHIER
(1902 – 1959)

SALLY FESTING

Newton-le-Willows

Published in the United Kingdom in 2021
by The Knives Forks And Spoons Press,
51 Pipit Avenue,
Newton-le-Willows,
Merseyside,
WA12 9RG.

ISBN 978-1-912211-86-9

Copyright © Sally Festing 2021.

The right of Sally Festing to be identified as the author of this work has been asserted by them in accordance with the Copyrights, Designs and Patents Act of 1988. All rights reserved. No part of this publication may be reproduced, stored in a retrieval system, transmitted in any form or by any means, electronic, photocopying, recording or otherwise, without prior permission of the publisher.

Acknowledgements:

My thanks to Peter Wallis, Moniza Alvi, Helena Nelson and Caroline Gilfillan for help with poems and layout, Stephen Eisenman for his expertise in the art world, Alice Crampin and Laura Davis for translations from French. Essays about Germaine Richier accompanied by poem excerpts are published in the 100th issue of *Acumen*, May 2021, and in Agenda online 'Pound' Supplement of 2020. Poems are in *Fenland Poetry Journal*, and earlier versions of 'Rook' and 'Fool' were published in *Poetry Review*.

A work of art can create no greater effect than when it transmits
the emotions that raged in the creator to the listener [viewer],
in such a way that they also rage and storm in him,
said composer Arnold Schoenberg.

CONTENTS

PREFACE	7
THE VINE-GROWER'S DAUGHTER	9
CAMARGUE	10
CREEPY-CRAWLIES	12
RATHER A SAVAGE CHILDHOOD	13
'WOMEN AREN'T MADE FOR ART'	14
L'ATELIER D'ANTOINE BOURDELLE	15
THE WORLD OF FORM	16
WAR	17
TOADWOMAN	19
HOMAGE TO SURVIVAL	20
DETHRONED	21
L'EAU	22
MATCH	23
LE MARI	24
THE COUPLE	25
ECHOES	26
L'ATELIER	27
CHECK BUT NOT MATE	29
ONE LAST GAME	30
CHESSBOARD	31
ROOK	32
KNIGHT	33
FOOL	34
KING	35
QUEEN	36
TIMELINE	37
NOTES	41

PREFACE

French Sculptor, Germaine Richier, was the first woman to be given a solo retrospective at the Musée National d'Art Moderne (in Paris, 1956). Following her early death, she was largely forgotten in the art world. But she had a few champions. In 1955, David Sylvester asserted that 'nobody perhaps occupies so central, so crucial a position in contemporary sculpture.'[1] He was right. 'Surely one of the most original sculptors of our century', echoed American critic and historian, Michael Gibson in 1996. 'Form and subject matter display a no-nonsense authenticity which deserves to be prized above all else.'[2] Such recognition came many years before her work began to feature in academic feminist studies. She was one of the very few women artists to receive international success in the 1940s and 1950s.

Richier's advocates included the poet Francis Pong, and the sculptors (and friends) Jean Arp, Alberto Giacometti, Marino Marini and Fritz Wotruba. Marini's *Head of Richier* (1945) is found in the Gallery of Modern Art in Milan. While it's often suggested that she's been overlooked because of her sex, Gibson, offered another explanation. "Richier's work has been both widely praised and generally neglected, mainly because it failed to fit into any established conservative or progressive movement." The truth must lie in a combination of the two. To Gibson, she was "one of the most original sculptors of our century.[3] As Winnicott says, 'It's joy to be hidden, disaster not to be found'.

I've been obsessed with Richier's work for a long time, looked at it in the Tate, read about the artist, and paid my respects by visiting the landscape that was seminal to her. On Sunday, 3 March 2003, I printed 'Stes Maries-de-la-Mer' across the page of my holiday-diary. *Wake from a siesta in the back of a Citroën parked round a stone-covered square. Hard-pollarded trees. Grubby white hotel.* The rest of the page was written outside in a wobbly hand. *Long grey beaches. Trees peppered with holes & striped with algae drift into weird beasts. Wedges of wood entombed in shifty, sifty sand. Great tufts of marram, flapping in the wind. Dead birds. Uprooted willows. Huge skies. Tamarisks. Perennial samphire. Sea purslane.*

The unexpected part: all these plants were familiar. It was a coincidence that the landscape of Richier's childhood had strong similarities with a spot on the North Norfolk coast that's part of mine. I swam in her sea and felt at home. The Camargue is, of course, more 'extreme', and this is a word Richier used about her work. Critics used it too. Through metamorphoses, one argued,[4] Richier appears to ask what lies at the extreme reaches of the human body.

Richier's sculpture became a point of reference for my poetry, Because of this, some diary jottings, and comments are woven between poems as well as in the four-page Timeline.

White Queen's Last Stand

THE VINE-GROWER'S DAUGHTER

Four siblings, rough-footed,
smelling of garlic, made plaited tracks
down wide grey shores.
    'Plus vite, Maine!
Our youngest looks at everything.'

Sun flushed the Midi.
Bird voices split the sky,
the wind took the land by the scruff of its neck.
Was she, like this delta,
    gorged with salt and water?

She cut runes in the sand –
'des étangs', littoral lines.
Drew circles with a stick.
    It's what kids do.
        What I did too, laying down bones

beside the slate-blue sea,
slipping into rituals of creation
when days were as long as the cockle path
    that threads through the saltings
to Scolt Head.

Every day with all our gear,
    and several times
when the water bottle was left behind,
I took a barefoot run
on mud-cracked hexagons.

The days were long.
    There was so much,
    so much time.

    Look! I made a perfect sun.
She balled her fists, signed GERMAINE.

Sally Festing
CAMARGUE

i.

Where sand blew back
                as the Mistral threw it,
she, most careful beachcomber
found a still recognizable flotsam buzzard
scraped and scoured
bitten and chewed.

The raptor's mask
                all beak and eye
lodged in her mind
with spilled littery shipwreck, wood drifted
from the Rhone – half-buried, stripped and peppered.
Pine transmogrified like bone.

ii.

The air was curdled with cries.
Teal and goldeneye quacked overhead
when she tenderly parted bamboos

to watch flamingos scoop crustaceans.
      Their legs are reed-skinny.
Necks contortionist-looped to water's skin.

Spoonbills with their squall of wings
got tossed
and mauled.

She was born where turbulence
washed the torn acres,
the sky contained its wrath –

wave cry, wind cry.
The mistral sang and sang
while the coypu coupled.

White Queen's Last Stand

iii.

My song questions Limonium,
a plant that's not quite
what it seems –

caspia / statice / sea lavender / marsh rosemary
spreads like a cloak
      woven out of wind

hiding the restless creeks
on a marsh that continually breaks
and builds again.

Here is home to the oyster-catcher's weeping –
they'll dive-bomb you when they have young;
the greylags, Brent, pink-footed geese.

Larks rise on its coastal path.
Fields full of peewits. Marram-twisted dunes.
Sunshine making merry the sea's extraordinary blue.

      But does Limonium deceive?
thrusting through aster, samphire, vast lichens,
covering the marsh's devils as if it reigned supreme.

Sally Festing
CREEPY-CRAWLIES

Dry-as-bone dust,
      sand made hollows where a girl could sit
her head buried in her coat against the sting.
The least insect was a gift
        and Germaine could name it,

her fingers were itchy for ant or mantis,
her ear was tuned to the cicada's buzz.
A mosquito fastened to her leg, blissfully
raised its abdomen. *Tu me piques.*
Blood sisters?

I was saying that when young, I consented to extra runs on the cockle path between precariously wobbly bridges of broken landfill, bearing a water-bottle (gifts) to the sand dunes where mother lay browning, sal volatile-soaked paper hankies tied to marram grass for horseflies. You hardly felt them settle just the sting before a huge red welt.

RATHER A SAVAGE CHILDHOOD

Words burst like small explosions
from her lips –

her first school, the downs,
her lessons the smell of thyme,
her master, the relentless sun.

The farm outside Montpellier,
where plane trees shaded silently
as the roots searched for cool.

Sometimes a harsh wind rang
through the leaves' profusions.

Light and darkness left their mark
on the bark of her shining giants.

Sally Festing

'WOMEN AREN'T MADE FOR ART'

Clearly she remembered what her father said
in Provencal as thick as hers'.
A blue-eyed man, high forehead, stern profile.

Montpellier's triumphal staircases,
Pérou walk, Jardin des Plants, its cedars,
and the planes' imperial dischord gripped her.

École des Beaux Arts
remembering what her father said,
she enrolled. And she grew strong

on possibility, a rearing horse, lit with light,
dragging her into dreams
      at every turn.

L'ATELIER D'ANTOINE BOURDELLE

Everything I know
I learned from him.

He spoke of balance and the axis.
'Fine to use compasses' he said,

'but learn to make them lie.
Put one thing in place. Proceed

from certainty.'
He taught me to analyse form.

Form is secreted by process, like our bodies. Form is secreted by experience, says improvisational musician Stephen Nachmanovitch.

There's a right time even for a fly when it proceeds from certainty. Like Beethoven, Richier found a guardian angel.

Sally Festing

THE WORLD OF FORM

i.

The Paris spring
            flickered.
The part of her head with a horse in it
                        galloped.

Marriage to a fellow sculptor. The studio near Bourdelle
in Avenue de Maine.

She sculpted *busts*, progressed to *figures*.
Every day she put clay on the framework,

muscular stuff,
and a whirlpool of likely failure.

She strove to honour what she loved,
to disturb what hung in the air.

ii.

She took a pupil to Pompeii. The pilgrimage
plumbed depths in her –

the blasted bodies,
architecture.

Flesh, pink and blind
lurked behind every echo.

iii.

Brussels, Paris – Exhibitions. Prizes.
New York.

She mixed with fellow sculptors,
Marini, Marko, Giacometti ...

all of them men
and the friends cross-fertilized.

WAR

Driven from home
she woke to upheaval
      in her husband's Switzerland
but the Valais region
    roused her
to create strange hybrids,
darn space
      with armatures.

As a child, she'd fostered grasshoppers,
    spiders, mantis, ants.
They rose from forest, reed beds, long grass,
    marshes, dunes, pools
            and they sang.
Shadows hatched and images streamed
      like insect traffic.
With *Sauterelle* (metamorphic hopper/woman)
    poised to spring
        they rose again.

The forest
      was like her dancing floor
its green
    opening her
to childhood – white poplar, ash and elm.
Trees were its bones.
Yellow iris,
water crowfoot
blooming in spring.

Challenged by the spoiled,
the humanoid, to grasp
necessary art
        and fix her figures
in other people's eyes,
she hauled in bark
to collage into clay
    with leaf and wood,

Sally Festing

so the dark
        of a hundred years
charged her,
        helped her to cast the *Forest Man*.
An arboreal creature –

halting step, suspended arms,
        wind-flayed,
                scabrous,
with one webbed hand.

A thistly starkness
filled her head – that raptor's mask
all beak and eye,
haunted the live and the dead.
She swallowed a bee
                pressed against her breast,
dreamed the distortions
                of war,
how it molested
        humans.

Our age is full of talons, people bristle, she said.
Wild things called to her,
 counterpart
              to the violence
                      of soldiers marching,
                            corpses in the forest.
She made strange forms
which, when they sang,
spat splinters of iron.

Derek Walcott said, the lines I love have all the knots left in.

White Queen's Last Stand

TOADWOMAN

She's toad in the leap   she is about   to spin

Toad in   her svelt skin's   perfect shine

in the slope of her back   plumped thighs   the joy of being alive

needing only   a slug to jog   her appetite

She's toad   in the feisty stretch   to the unknown

Before writing these poems, I photocopied a large number of illustrations of her work from photos by Brassai for an exhibition at Galerie Berggruen in San Francisco in 1956. I've looked at them constantly.

Le Crepaud takes me to the natterjack toad once found on our seawall – to the excitement of four children who were with me. It had a distinctive yellow line, warty skin and iridescent eyes.

In a similar way, Richier's *La Chauve-souris* prompts me to the high-pitched evening calls of pipistrelle and long-eared bats, black against fading light in late summer. To the baby bat we rescued and fed milk from a pipette. Released the next morning it made an extraordinary vertical climb with its wingclaws, straight up wall of the house and into the eaves.

Sally Festing

HOMAGE TO SURVIVAL

Back in Paris   her shoulders broad as river banks
she was stocky, with rough-cropped hair,
      a direct gaze and steady hands

clawing back a semblance of the human form
with heavy-worked surfaces, distortions,
and pock-marked flesh.

We ... cannot conceal, she said,
*human expression
in the drama of our time.*

Hurricane Woman's hefty body might have been modelled on her own,
infused with wind-whipped conflict –
tense muscles, frightened fingers, scarred flesh.

Its counterpart, *Storm Man,*
is a naked male about to step
from his thin, rough-bronzed base.

Rawness is caught in the compressed power
of his rugged stance, distended belly.
His mutilated face suggests

directions of her own. Germaine felt childhood
slipping beneath the present in cycles of change and decay,
in the cries swung on air, of hawk and pike after prey.

She felt the wavecrests' crash and stole their motion,
seeing survival in a game
where all evolved and flamed.

DETHRONED

'There is no face' they cried.
Her bronze hung stark on its cross.
Resilient. Christ survived.

*'There is no cross. How can your Christ
be crucified?'*

Hot blue light bore down the Alpine sky.
Richier's crucifix for the Chapel of Assy
was a daring commission,

an unsettling
         and hurtful one,
she tried to forget.

The cross is taken into flesh, she said.
The wood is hidden by his arms.

She suffered when the Bishop of Annecy
ordered it removed from its *mise en scène*.

She knew, after all, her Christ, if harsh, was beautiful.
Christ is God is spirit. Faceless
is the nature of God.

Seven years later, still sensitive about the humiliating reaction to her work, Richier was, nevertheless, able to re-assess: *All these people who came out violently on one side or the other, it goes well with my sculpture ... We southerners look cheerful, but beneath the surface a drama is buried. Arles is a tragic town. The women go out walking in wintertime with black shawls drawn around their heads.*[5]

Sally Festing
L'EAU

Say she's *Water,* her neck an amphora found on the beach,
Stes Maries de la Mer.
Headless. Battered. How sturdily she sits,
skinny limbs stressing her body's volume,
      for she's also a source of life,
a vessel that swallowed the sun,
a survivor with vestigial wings.
Beneath and around her, nature is contained.

Say her first man lumbered off,
like *Shepherd* on metal wires,
lean geometric counterpoints
to support he'd given for more than twenty years.

Was her mettle then, too much for him?
Three Venice Biennales and a star at Sao Paulo.
Ruthless schedules. Childlessness.
No eyes, her head's on fire, but such a thirst.
So much water pouring to the rough rude sea.
Did her heart burst?
She knew vessels, she knew water,
      she knew mortal thirst.

MATCH

She played an ancient game
                         and moved the pieces.
Man of Night slipped in, winged, bat-headed,
gripped the earth with leaden paws to keep him bound.
Alleluia! Lose one, gain one;
       feet on the ground.
Her new man said, *'she's a wild thing'*.

Marianne Moore wrote, *We must have the courage of our peculiarities.*

Richier didn't need to find her 'inner clown', it was already within her – a wellspring of creative force that left her alive and free.

Sally Festing
LE MARI

Night was when her hands grew huge, and Germaine
felt the tug of love, the lunge of passion.
With so much nakedness left inside her,
she rummaged her body for angles, gesture,
dreamt of forest-bark, paw, claw, woods.
Leaning sideways, backwards, forwards,
(contradiction tests reality said Simone Weil),
she navigated as if they were one flesh,
alive to his rebellion, the hex
of his words, his touch, the fur on his skin, his sex.

'Main' he called her, his virtue coursing through
her womb and breast. Balance, her goddess, drew
her, pouring what goes on between sea and sands
into her monstrously strong and willing hands.

THE COUPLE

They sound each other, bounce off the other,
feet off the ground. In violent
union, they're holding hands –
their legs attenuated, their bodies distended,
equilibrium precarious. He sings
to bind him to the earth, brings her myths,
wakes a pageant of forms
beyond the reaches of her bones.

Beyond the reaches of her bones,
he wakes a pageant of forms,
sings to bind him to the earth, brings her myths.
Their equilibrium is precarious,
their bodies distended, legs attenuated.
They're holding hands in union
that's violent. Feet off the ground,
they bounce off each other, each sounds the other.

John Cage said that he was not interested in art as self-expression but as self-alteration.

Sally Festing

ECHOES

In Bouches-du-Rhone again,
she remembered
early morning, the dawn coming up
under dusky skies, flotsam, beachcombing,
foraging for wood
                  when marram stripped
her legs and stung. The hungry miles,
four of them running like wild white horses
coralling black bulls.
Toads sang. Sun blinded their eyes.

What she remembered was long afternoons'
lyrical rhythms when heat shimmered
off the dunes, when hoppers gathered
in her hair, when a dead fox
                            decomposing
in the shallows lay gutted
                              close to its lair.
The beauty of wreckage, when spray
sparked trinkets of glass. When waves broke
in a million endings and darkness fell.

What she remembered
was evenings
when a muted sun gave way to stars,
when she lived outside, cried like a night owl;
when bats' echolocation bounced the air,
and the sky, being a darkish olive-green,
made an oversized chessboard of marsh
and sand that focused her mind
as stars came out.
And shadows closed in.

L'ATELIER

The workbench is bolted with its vice –
two jaws. The grip. Compasses

hang from a bar, a stove barrel-like bulges,
telephone's clay-shamed.

This is her belly, her womb,
where young are conceived and grown.

See the newborn staged in every corner.
Battle is waged, the studio crammed.

*

This is her world with her figures.
It varies – she laughs. Despairs.

When the hole in her gut feels small
and the sun shines in, she gives them buddings.

When the hurricane whistles through,
she knows what it's like and punctures.

Witch in a warehouse, she challenges family
until skin-scrapes cake her hair.

*

In husky Provencal, she sings.
Savageness nurtures metamorphosis.

A lizard expires and becomes bronze.
Clay weaves its fingers into hers

and pulls her to its heart.
Day after day in her womb

Sally Festing

she chases between sky and sea.
Before pain prevails, each quickening –

La Mante, La Sauterelle, Storm Man, Hurricane ...

Poet Anghlaki-Rooke always questioned how her body would react 'to the weather, to aging, to sickness, to a storm, to love? The highest ideas, the loftiest concepts, depend on the morning cough …' [6]

One may wonder whether this is not the highly specific way this energetic, strong-willed woman, who had no children beside her sculptures, found of representing her femininity.[7]

CHECK BUT NOT MATE

The sea swept turbulent,
healed her face and hands.

She was a tiny creature,
blood, guts and eye sockets. Dried bones.

The stars blinked languidly,
in the pitiless skies.

Grappling with cancer,
what could she do

but burn like driftwood
brilliantly.

Brooding on her chessmen –
Rook, Knight, Fool, King, Queen,

she built life-size simulacrums
gave them gesture.

On another visit to the Tate, I stood in front of *Chessboard (Grande)* with a plain sheet of paper fixed to a plastic folder. Moving round the sculptures, I made pencil sketches of them. Then with felt-tips in deep blue, red, green and yellow, I copied in the radiant lines that course through various nerves, arteries and bones of the figures. Only red marks the *Knight* who appears to me a network of nervy vessels. The *King* has prominent red lungs and heart, his limbs and the callipers he carries are green and blue, his stomach is green. Like *Knight*, he lacks the merest touch of the sunny yellow enjoyed by *Rook, Queen and Fool*. The French call their chess Bishop 'le fou' or fool. Fool is covered in bold modern shapes, a mass of contradictions. *Queen* is deeply, feelingly, multicoloured around stomach and womb.

Sally Festing

ONE LAST GAME

Convalescing
      where Mistrals dragged Mireille across the moor,
she reflected on her forms.

How dark it was in a sombre patch,
filling cloud-distance mile after mile.

Trying to catch the sun, aching to stay Grandmaster,
she wandered after a bird, a voyager. Bewitched.

Should she paint her giant chessmen brilliant pigments,
follow the heart, the nerves, the bones.

Colour distracts, but then why not?
A remedy for pain.

The wind blubbered her mouth,
looned its threat in a current of cold.

Passing sailors could be more cruel
than the storm.

Has the White Queen lost her way?
among waves. The weariness.

There was no defence.
She just kept playing, mastering, as she

stepped into distress. Comrade with the owl,
in Germaine, evening would find itself.

Richier's work was still in my mind on a trip to New York's MOMA. Beside a rough diagram of Paul Klee's *Rider*, I wrote *unhorsed and bewitched. She is on a journey, wandering after a bird.*

White Queen's Last Stand

CHESSBOARD

*Queen, King, Knight, Rook, Fool,
she pushed them on stage,
forces prepared for threat and defence.
Threat and defence.*

Art (if we want to use the word with a certain intensity) suggests something beyond itself. We cannot be finished with it. says Nachmanovitch.

Sally Festing

ROOK
from Old French roc(k)

You're a crock, a crumble. A veteran.
An amputee (no hands).

No diagonal vision,
you lurch towards the farthest shore,

Home is the corner where you limp and croak for alms.
Nights camped beneath the Tamarisk's pink blossom,

a fatal move.
Charity they say, toss you a coin.

KNIGHT

It's a dragon. No a giraffe.
It's just been born. Doesn't have front legs.

Like a seahorse,
a confection of bird-bright
hints and clues.
Maybe a fish-fly with blue silk fins.

Like quicksilver
you kick up your heels –
a jagged cut or a race through waves
to assist your friends.

Sally Festing
FOOL

An O without a figure
you're one half painted egg

    the other half a fireball
    dipping the horizon

Your pink eye signals caution

    your green eye says go
    scoot the diagonal

An O without a figure
you can't catch and cradle

    hide crosier and charism
    for laying-on-of-hands

You watch how the wind cuts
it often breaks your heart

    You creep about the ward
    dispensing pills

You embarrass yourself

    sob softly   nurse suffering

Dissident in motley

    a capering automaton

You refuse to battle

    just tip your campanulate cap
    and wag your tail

KING

Sometimes you're threatened
scared of capture

You risk letting beach sand
burn your face

Backwards   forwards   sideways
stiffly   one step
          at a time

your callipers quiver
when you dream

Subtly you defend your troops
but powerless   can you protect the Queen?

Sally Festing
QUEEN

Grandmother you gallop from a field stamped black
gripping your mare trident in one hand

Tallest you've a cow's skull belly pierced back torn

You count your beads carry on dodging the thistles
rattling chains to Poseidon You refuse to be unsung

TIMELINE

Germaine Richier (1902-1959) was born in Gras, Bouches-du-Rhône and frequently expressed her debt to the neighbourhoods of Arles, Saintes Maries-de-la-mer and Montpellier in the Languedoc for inspiration.

After six years at the École des Beaux Arts in Montpellier, she moved to Paris, a private pupil of Antoine Bourdelle. In 1929 she married the Swiss sculptor Otto Bänninger, Bourdelle's director and assistant, acknowledging later, *it's Bänninger who brought me into art and it is to him that I owe emancipation from my bourgeois life.*

Her talent was recognized early. Various achievements throughout the 30s included a solo exhibition in 1934, the Blumenthal Prize for Sculpture, work shown at the Paris World's Fair 1937, and an international exhibition in New York the following year in company with Pierre Bonnard, George Braque, Marc Chagall, Robert Delaunay, Andre Derain and Jacques Lipchitz. World War Two ended an especially happy decade. Work, work, she could never have enough. She was in her studio from dawn until evening when she joined her circle in Montparnasse to talk or visit exhibitions.

The War took her to Zurich, her husband's former home. Until then, her work was classical, henceforth, her individuality progressed rapidly. *Le Crapaud* (*Toad* 1940) was an early expression of her allegorical interest in the animal world. A woman kneels back, one foot on her toes, her back a silky twist, right arm stretched as if caught in forward motion. *Le Crepaud* was precursor to a string of hybrid animal/human/ insect mutants she made off and on to the end of her life.

La Sauterelle, La Mante and *L'Araignée* (grasshopper/locust, ant and spider) all have female breasts and a deeply creased and puckered skin. *La Sauterelle* sits on a short pedestal almost streamlined with the forward lurch of the body, arms bent at the elbows, hands stretched, fingers splayed in readiness to leap. *La Mante* is suitably emaciated, the feet extended into wiry, stippled bronze curves. Precariousness is emphasised above all in the gesture of arms and large, downward-pointing fingers. *L'Araignée* grabs a geometry of wires, setting up powerful tension between its limbs. 'The "women-insects" are not objects of the eroticizing male gaze but deformed and macabre creatures with bodies that have lived and experienced, and are still ploughing on.'[8] *Bat, Bird-Man* and others were to follow.

A fruitful corollary of Richier's forest walks made during the Occupation, was renewed affinity with the grammar of her birthplace. The old spell of trees changed the direction of her work, and she asked her elder brother (with whom she was always especially close), to send her the branch of an olive tree from home. Real bark, as well as a large leaf she found in the Swiss Valais region were collaged onto the clay before casting *Forest Man* (1945).

October 1946 saw her return to Paris where she felt the foundation of her working life lay. *It seems to me that in violent* (sculptures) *there is just as much wisdom as in poetic ones*, she said. This was many years before Louise Bourgeois produced sculpture that invoked our worst nightmares. In Paris, Richier re-established links with many old friends, artists and intellectuals as well as literati such as Nathalie Sarraute and Colette. At this juncture, historian poet René de Solier, became her companion and constant support.

At the École, Richier had studied under one of Rodin's former assistants. Later, she hired the Master's model, Nardone, for *Storm Man (1947-8);* thereby sharing the tradition for monumental bronze. She may well have fostered dialogues with past masters in order to promote her work. With visitors, her light touch tended to counter her bluntness. *I made people pose a great deal. Ninety sittings sometimes. I had to have the model at my mercy.*

In 2019, *Storm Man* stood beside a doorway in a Liz Frink exhibition in the Sainsbury Centre for Visual Arts. In shadowless light how he vibrated! He is immortal. Richier's reverence was embalmed in the beaten metal of wind-pummelled sculpture that followed the anguish of war.

Her commission for a *Crucifix* (1950) for the church of Assy was a testing one. Quickly, she made a preliminary model, saying *I want the result of a concept, a knowledge, a dare, all of it, if possible, very alive [...] I don't envisage a sculpture of several months' work, I want to go there directly if possible*. The religious controversy that ensued was an embarrassment, although lifelong Catholic Francois Mauriac admired her Christ and a critic pronounced it, 'One of the rare modern crucifixes to appear artistically convincing'.[9]

In 1951 she left Otto Bänninger. Three years later, she married de Solier. The latter had signed a petition against the Algerian war. For a woman described as having 'untamable will',[10] he was a happy match. Solier commented to a friend how exceptional he believed Richier's sculpture was. She returned *He is a very magnificent man ... If I had the words, I'd be a writer. Le Couple* (1954) was her way of celebrating.

L'Eau (1953) is cast, appropriately, in dark grey patinated bronze. *They made thick legs when sculpture had a respect for the canon,* Richier said. *This I do not care to maintain.*

The head of *Shepherd of the Landes* (1951) is cast from eroded building rubble. In the Landes region of southern France the shepherds used stilts to help them view their sheep over large areas of scrub and marsh. Richier's figure is not only on stilts but is one with them.

She was also incorporating into her work pieces that might have been thrown up on the beach near the mouth of the Petit Rhône; driftwood, olive branches, as well as tools used to cultivate the soil and objects of Provençal folklore. All reflected life in the area. *Ant's Head* (1953) was made from a three-pronged goad used by 'guardians' who cared for the wild horses and bulls of the Camargue.

De Solier's references to process, highlight the physicality of his wife's vocation. 'Patina is another major problem for the sculptor', he told a journalist.[11] 'The patina-maker brushes on the acid and burns it with a blow-pipe. It's dreadful work'.

Alongside Reg Butler, Bernard Meadows and Eduardo Paolozzi, Richier was a source for British artists associated with the 'geometry of fear'. Sculptures such as *Don Quichotte* (1951) were influenced by abstract art. *Man of the Night* (1954) resembles a bird as much as human form.

The year after her solo retrospective in Paris, she had her first solo in New York City.

She took risks, experimenting with ceramics, mosaic, and printmaking. In 1947 she first tried engraving. Later, she made figures in lead. In 1951 she illustrated Arthur Rimbaud's *Illuminations* with watercolours. Four years after her second marriage she illustrated de Solier's poems, *Contre Terre* (1958).

One of my Diary entries notes: *In chess, an expert player seems to see the lines of force and influence on a board.* In the last four years of her life, Richier returned tirelessly to *Chessboard* (1955-9) a group of five anthropomorphic figures. The original smaller-scale figures were modelled in clay and plastiline arranged on a board of scrap iron. The larger, plaster version was modelled by a technician in April 1959 (soon after she returned to Paris from Montpellier) before being cast in plaster and painted. This was three months before she died. Mounted on pale, free-standing pedestals and spindly legged, they buckle under the strain of their own distended bodies, presenting a far more precarious equilibrium than the small version.

Sally Festing

She had made sculptures set against abstract backgrounds created by painters Maria Elena Vieira da Silva, Hans Hartung, and Zao Wou-ki. She had tried using coloured glass, and in 1956 she enameled the natural bronze surface of a few pieces. Whether to use paint directly on her Chess pieces remained, she owned, a difficult decision. *In this business of colours, perhaps I'm wrong, perhaps I'm right. I don't know at all. What I do know is that, in all cases, it pleases me. Sculpture is serious, colour is cheerful. I want my statues to be cheerful, active. Normally, a colour on a sculpture is distracting. But, after all, why not?*[12]

Rook (Castle) is the most abstracted chess piece, with three legs to a vertically elongated body extending upwards in reed-like sticks. A short horizontal protuberance mid-body could be penile.

Knight combines a horse's head with an insect's thorax.

Fool's face is recognizably human. His egg-like body sports a short protruding tail.

King's head is a branched plant form, his callipers invaluable sculpting tools. His protruding belly sports an enlarged belly button.

Queen's cattle-face goes weirdly with realistic human buttocks. In one hand, like *Ant's Head*, she carries a trident. Poseidon struck a rock with his divine instrument.

Richier's much earlier *Storm Man* had a wide, deep gash for a navel. *Queen* has a hole that pierces right through her body, emphasizing vulnerability. Richier said, *What characterizes a sculpture is the way in which it renounces a solid, full form. Holes and perforations light up the material, which then becomes organic and open ... it is through there (holes) that the light passes. A form cannot exist without expression. And one cannot deny human expression as making up part of the drama of our time.*[13]

NOTES

[1] David Sylvester, *On Germaine Richier*, p. 2 (Germaine Richier: Exhibition of Sculpture) Hanover Gallery, London: 1955.

[2] Michael Gibson, 'Germaine Richier, an Original', *The New York Times*, 4th May 1996.

[3] ibid.

[4] Natalie Ferris, 'Tate Modern lives of the Artists 81', (DPhil thesis on abstraction in post-war British literature, Queen's College, University of Oxford, 2019).

[5] Paul Guth, 'Encounter with Germaine Richier', *Yale French Studies, Contemporary Art 19/20*, (1957).

[6] Katerina Anghelaki-Rooke 'Three Poems translated from the Greek by Karen Van Dyck', *PNR 252 Vol.46, No 4 March-April 2020*.

[7] Gibson.

[8] Marine Picard, *2019*. 'MA Research Thesis in Art History' (The Open University, Milton Keynes, 2019).

[9] Gibson.

[10] Guth (also some of the quotes by Richier).

[11] ibid.

[12] ibid.

[13] ibid.